THE
RED HORSE

WAR AGAINST GOD'S GOVERNMENT

CONNIE ORDELHEIDE-ANDERSON

WESTBOW·
PRESS
A DIVISION OF THOMAS NELSON
& ZONDERVAN

WestBow Press books may be ordered through booksellers or by contacting:

WestBow Press
A Division of Thomas Nelson & Zondervan
1663 Liberty Drive
Bloomington, IN 47403
www.westbowpress.com
1 (866) 928-1240

Scripture taken from the King James Version of the Bible.

ISBN: 978-1-4908-2488-8 (sc)
ISBN: 978-1-4908-2487-1 (e)

Printed in the United States of America.

WestBow Press rev. date: 05/02/2014

INTRODUCTION TO BIBLE SYMBOLS

"It is the glory of God to conceal a thing: but the honor of kings is to search out a matter." (Proverbs 25:2).

Symbols are a part of our society. Where words change Bible symbols remain the same. Prophets spoke then repeated themselves expanding their thoughts. This created added value to a symbol and created what I call a *prophetic function*. For instance the text below we have the words, days, voice, angel, seventh, mystery, God, servants, sound, begin, declared, finished and prophets.

The Bible must explain its own symbols. A Bible word search may give you a word like fish. But Jesus said, "I will make you fishers of men," not fish. Fishermen may catch a sea creature. God catches us with His Holy Spirit but that does not change God or his Government. He may make you the bait!

"But in the days of the voice of the seventh angel, when he shall begin to sound, **the mystery of God should be finished,** as he has declared to his servants the prophets." (Revelation 10:7).

These mysteries are for us *in the days* the very last days of earth's history. Listen for the change of *voice* in Bible poetry. Words can be literal like the number seven. However seven is also a number with a *spiritual meaning* that points us to our creator who completed his work of creating in six days and **rested on the seventh day.** *Seven* is a number and perfection. **The seventh angel completes the mystery of God.** Listen for the change of *who is sounding* what? God is not silent, he is thundering from Heaven like he did on Mount Sinai. He invites us to search out a matter.

eBook best viewed in two pages scrolling.

THE CREATOR NOTICED REBELLION IN HIS KINGDOM: A created human like robot began to undermine the Government of God. Rebellion vexed the Spirit of God. Lucifer wanted to sit on God's Throne and be God.

GOD'S SOLUTION: Give Lucifer a created being and his angels, time and space, to prove they can create and manage our planet without moral boundaries. (How is that working for you?)

PLAN: The Blood Sacrifice of God the Son, would prove beyond a shadow of doubt, his blood is alien, with twenty four chromosomes of living blood a fact since 1982, ask a Jew.

RULES: The Creator must abide by His Laws he wrote in rock on Mount Sinai. Lucifer can lie, steal, cheat and think to change the times and Laws of God.

TIME LIMIT: Approximately six thousand years.

JUDGMENT OF EVIL: Ultimately the Heavenly Courts make a unanimous vote for Michael over Lucifer. (Daniel 7: 25-27).

OUTCOME: Everyone is granted Freedom purchased by the Son of God to obey or not obey His Commandments.

NO EXCULSIONS: "If we say that we have no sin, we deceive ourselves, and the truth is not in us." (1 John 1:8). Adam and Eve brought a death sentence on created beings, in committing the original sin of disobedience against Jesus Christ their Creator.

REALITY: The World's longest prophecy proves the Bible is true. On 9-11-2001 a 2300 year prophecy ended that began in 457 B.C. with the decree of Artaxerxes. Jesus moved out of the Holy Place in Heaven, to enter the Most Holy, as Our High Priest in 1844 exactly 2300 years since 457 B.C. His blood and mercy is now seen as the only blood sacrifice that can redeem us. 9-11-2001 ends the Last Day of Atonement in Heaven- The principle is found in Isaiah 63:10, "But they rebelled, and vexed his holy Spirit: therefore he was turned to be their enemy, *and* he fought against them."

GOD IS RARELY SILENT: The day he watched his son die at the Place of the Skull, Golgotha God was silent! He knew how few contemplated the meaning of His suffering and the suffering of His Son. Freedom is not free! Jesus purchased your freedom of choice with His blood, on Calvary. Follow HIS WORD in Revelation 8:1.

CHAPTER I

OUR STORY BEGINS IN HEAVEN
THE LAMB OF GOD OPENS THE 7ᵀᴴ SEAL

"And when he had opened the seventh seal, there was silence in heaven for about half an hour." (Revelation 8:1).

"And one of the elders saith unto me, Weep not: behold, the Lion of the tribe of Judah, the Root of David, hath prevailed to open the book, and to loose the seven seals thereof. [Jesus Christ]

"And I beheld, and, lo, in the midst of the throne and of the four beasts, and in the midst of the elders, stood a Lamb as it had been slain, having seven horns and seven eyes, which are the seven Spirits of God sent forth into all the earth. (Revelation 5:5,6).

Imagine a Courtroom the size of an Olympic Stadium with a round table discussion with twenty four human beings, four beasts ready to speak up in behalf of God and seven Holy Spirits surrounding the scene about to take orders to sound the Ram's Horn, announcing the wrath of God has begun.

SEPTEMBER 11, 2001 OPENED NEW LIGHT FROM SCRIPTURES

Thus far,
the heavenly courts
have been portrayed as filled
with praise and song. Now all is silent in
awesome expectancy of the things that are about
to occur. So understood, this silence of the seventh seal forms
a bridge between the opening of the seals and the blowing of
the trumpets, for it implies
that with
the seventh
seal *the
revelation
is not
complete-*
there is still
more to be
explained
concerning
God's program
Of events in the
great controversy with evil.

The silence in Heaven **brings new light on the Righteousness of Jesus Christ.** Seven is the number of completion with God. He created earth in six literal days, rested and blessed the 7th day, making it holy. Jesus moved into the Most Holy place in the Heavenly Sanctuary in 1844, exactly 2300 years from 457 B.C. that began with the decree of Artaxerxes in 457 B.C. Jesus, the sacrifice, became Jesus Our High Priest. Jesus began to **cleanse the sins confessed on the head of Jesus, the Lamb of God and turns to put the sins of the world on the head of His arch enemy the real Scapegoat Lucifer.** On 9-11-2001 Lucifer saw he was divorced, by all of Heaven. His bitterness and anger turned to get revenge on God. Lucifer is waging war against God's Government and your freedom of conscience.

SEVEN ANGELS SENT TO THE SEVEN CHURCHES

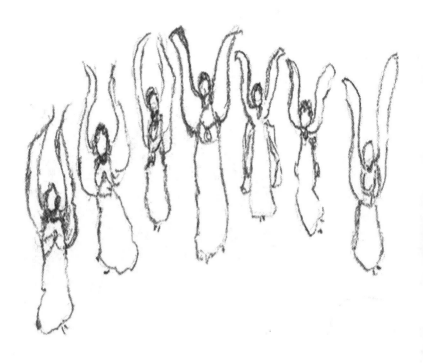

"And I saw the seven angels who stood before God;
and to them were given seven trumpets."
(Revelation 8:2).

"The mystery of the seven stars which thou sawest in my right hand, and the seven golden candlesticks. **The seven stars are the angels of the seven churches:** and the seven candlesticks which thou sawest are the seven churches." (Revelation 1:20).

SEVEN ANGELS COME TO THE SEVEN CHURCHES

Seven holy angels are sent to seven churches in Revelation two and three with unique personalities. Seven is the number of perfection and completion. God is completing his work of revealing himself as Our Creator.

Jesus the seventh angel walks through the seven churches to examine and critique each one in Revelation two and three:

"I know thy works, and thy labor, and thy patience, and how thou canst not bear them which are evil: and thou hast tried them which say they are apostles, and are not, and hast found them liars:" (Revelation 2:2)

"Nevertheless, I have a few things against you: You have people there who hold to the teaching of Balaam, who taught Balak to entice the Israelites to sin by committing sexual immorality."(Revelation 2:14) [Balaam taught adultery against God.]

"Likewise you also have those who hold to teaching of the Nicolaitans." [men who tried to control the conscience of those beneath them.]" (Revelation 2:15)

"So hast thou also them that hold the doctrine of the Nicolaitans, which thing I hate. Repent; or else I will come unto thee quickly, and *will fight against them with the sword of my mouth*." Revelation 2:15-16)

"Nevertheless I have *somewhat* against thee, *because thou hast left thy first love*. Remember therefore from whence thou art fallen, and repent, and do the first works; or else I will come unto thee quickly, and will remove thy candlestick out of his place, **except thou repent.** (Revelation 2:4-5).

"Fear none of those things which thou shalt suffer: behold, the devil shall cast *some* of you into prison, that ye may be tried; and ye shall have tribulation ten days: be thou faithful unto death, and I will give thee a crown of life." (Revelation 2:10)

Man Meets God At The Altar In Heaven
You have entered his Throne Room in Orion

"**And another angel came** and stood at the altar, having a golden censer; and there was given unto him much incense, that he should offer it with the prayers of all saints upon the golden altar which was before the throne." (Revelation 8:3).

Heaven is open and **you are standing in God's Courtroom.** Happy to say, **Gods Government has been judge by a unanimous vote, and found to be the Government chosen by the inhabitants of the Universe.** "I beheld, and the same horn made war with the saints, and prevailed against them; Until the Ancient of days came, **and judgment was given to the saints of the most High; and the time came that the saints possessed the kingdom.** Thus he said, The fourth beast shall be the fourth kingdom upon earth, which shall be diverse from all kingdoms, and shall devour the whole earth, and shall tread it down, and break it in pieces. And the ten horns out of this kingdom *are* ten kings *that* shall arise: and another shall rise after them; and he shall be diverse from the first, and he shall subdue three kings. **And he shall speak *great* words against the most High, and shall wear out the saints of the most High, and think to change** times and laws: and they shall **be given into his hand until a time and times and the dividing of time.** But the judgment shall sit, and **they shall take away his dominion, to consume and to destroy** *it* **unto the end**. And the kingdom and dominion, and the greatness of the kingdom under the whole heaven, shall be given to the people of the saints of the most High, whose kingdom *is* an everlasting kingdom, and all dominions shall serve and obey him. Daniel 7:21-27).)

"Behold, the days come, saith the LORD, **that I will make a new covenant** with the house of Israel, and with the house of Judah: Not according to the covenant that I made with their fathers in the day *that* I took them by the hand to bring them out of the land of Egypt; **which my covenant they brake**, although **I was an husband unto them, saith the LORD:** But this *shall be* the covenant that I will make with the house of Israel; After those days, saith the LORD, **I will put my law in their inward parts, and write it in their hearts; and will be their God, and they shall be my people.** And they shall teach no more every man his neighbour, and every man his brother, saying, Know the LORD: for they shall all know me, from the least of them unto the greatest of them, saith the LORD: **for I will forgive their iniquity, and I will remember their sin no more.** Thus saith the LORD, which giveth the sun for a light by day, *and* the ordinances of the moon and of the stars for a light by night, which divideth the sea when the waves thereof roar; **The LORD of hosts** *is* **his name**: If those ordinances depart from before me, saith the LORD, *then* the seed of Israel also shall cease from being a nation before me for ever. Thus saith the LORD; If heaven above can be measured, and the foundations of the earth searched out beneath, I will also cast off all the seed of Israel for all that they have done, saith the LORD. (Jeremiah 31:31-37).

"And I will give them one heart, and **I will put a new spirit within you;** and I will take the stony heart out of their flesh, and **will give them an heart of flesh that they may walk in my statutes, and keep mine ordinances, and do them: and they shall be my people, and I will be their God.**" (Ezekiel 11:19-20.).

THE NAIL SCARED HAND OF JESUS HOLDS OUR PRAYERS

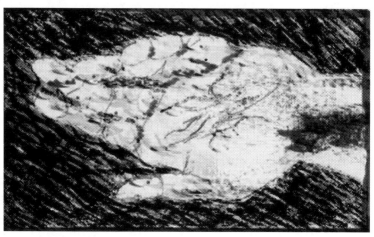

"And the smoke of the incense, which came with the prayers of the saints, ascended up before God *out of the angel's hand*" (Revelation 8: 3-4).

Imagine Jesus holding your prayers in His nail pierced hand. Incense represents our prayers. As we confess our sins, return what we have stolen, and admit we have born false witness about his Kingdom of Truth, this makes a sweet smell to the nose of Jesus! God and the heavenly beings are glorified! They see *you have gained wisdom.*

There were times when Jesus had to carry you. There were times when he cried with you. Those are the times you came to understand, his suffering, his love, his anxiety for you, the night he said, "Let this cup pass from me." When we feel down and out, we know Jesus felt the same way, in giving up his life to save us. Jesus says, "How can I give you up?" "What more could do I?" He pruned the tree, and the roots reached out to the Holy Spirit. They wanted to be connected to the vine. Jesus needs someone to hold him up like the pillars in front of the Sanctuary. A vine produces the fruit. Grapes that lay on the ground soon produce sour, fermented grapes.

Jesus said, "Beware of the yeast of the Pharisees." Pure unadulterated truth comes from the source of truth. For every good thing God gave Adam and Eve they made one mistake against God and we can testify we all know more about good and evil than we want to know! What does God hear in our prayers?

"And when he had opened the fifth seal, I saw under the altar the souls of them that were slain for the word of God, and for the testimony which they held: And they cried with a loud voice, saying, How long, O Lord, holy and true, dost thou not judge and avenge our blood on them that dwell on the earth? And white robes were given unto every one of them; and it was said unto them, that they should rest yet for a little season, until their fellow servants also and their brethren, that should be killed as they were, should be fulfilled. (Revelation 6:9-11).

Jesus makes us rest. There are disciples dying to self, preparing themselves, repenting, and finding themselves to be the one God is waiting for. Some have not put on the Robe of His Righteousness. They are wolves in lambs clothing, pretending to be obedient to God and man. This is the time before you see Jesus coming in the clouds, to bow down to God, repent and return what you have stolen, like Zacchaeus. Zacchaeus returned four times what he had stolen, because Jesus came to eat at his house. Jesus saw in the money changer a man who wanted to be treated with dignity and respect. A little short man wanted to be recognized by Jesus, so he climbed up into a tree, so he could see Jesus passing by.

"And grieve not the holy Spirit of God, whereby ye are sealed unto the day of redemption." (Ephesians 4:30).

"He therefore that despiseth, despiseth not man, but God, who hath also given unto us his holy Spirit." (1Thessalonians 4:8).

The best smell to God and Jesus is the confession of your faith that leads to repentance, and turning away from her, Babylon, the false city, the false church, the false mother.

COALS OF FIRE ARE THROWN DOWN THAT RESPRESENT THE HOLY SPIRIT ENDING THE LAST DAY OF ATONEMENT IN HEAVEN OUR BRIDEGROOM IS COMING!

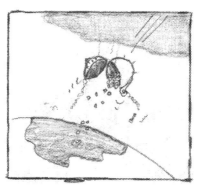

"And the angel took the censer, and filled it with fire from the altar, and cast it into the earth: and there were voices, and thundering's, and lightening's, and an earthquake." (Revelation 8:5).

"And it shall come to pass in the last days, saith God, I will pour out of my Spirit upon all flesh: and your sons and your daughters shall prophesy, and your young men shall see visions, and your old men shall dream dreams:" (Act 2:17)

"Howbeit when he, the Spirit of truth, is come, he will guide you into all truth: for he shall not speak of himself; but whatsoever he shall hear, that shall he speak: and he will shew you things to come." (John 16:13).

"Verily, verily, I say unto you, He that believeth on me, the works that I do shall he do also; and greater works than these shall he do; because I go unto my Father." (John14:12).

In 1989 the Berlin Wall came down, the Iron Curtain dropped in Russia, and on Tiananmen Square in China a man fought for liberty of speech in a dual with an armored tank, to the death. In revenge to destroy and discredit God, Lucifer was behind the fall of the Twin Towers in USA, as predicted by his Prophetess in 1903.

THE ABOMINATION OF DESOLATION CAUSED BY THE SCAPEGOAT REVEALS LUICER HAS FALLEN INTO HIS OWN TRAP

The scapegoat Lucifer is stuck in quicksand. He has been *judged, as the cause of all sin, sickness, and death in our world.* This poor creature used all his power to deceive the very elect. His name is Lucifer THE DESTROYER of everything good! He has trapped more men in his sand trap by convincing men to "Just blame God!"

If God didn't make all those rules everything would be O.K. God turns to be the enemy of Lucifer and his angels. Lucifer mixes the drinks that mix sexual immorality with truth.

Lucifer gloats! "Jesus will die for you, like he did for Mel Gibson! Just nail Jesus an innocent Jew to The Cross, for your sin, like Mel Gibson did! Do you see the irony? Without God there is no good or evil, so nail an innocent Jew to the cross, just like the Jews did in their day. If we are not careful we will be crucifying Jesus Christ like the Jews did.

On the Last Day of Atonement in Heaven, God points a finger at the real Scapegoat, Lucifer, the unseen enemy of God. The fires in the earth are being heated up for Lucifer and his angels.

You see Jews have a fear of having sin in their heart. At the end of the year they will not be blessed, if they continue to sin. They confess their sins, before midnight! They crown God as their King for a New Year! They renew their covenant vows to be obedient less the curse comes down on their own heads.

A Blessing Or Curse!

And after these things **I saw another angel come down from heaven, having great power; and the earth was lightened with his glory. And he cried mightily with a strong voice,** saying, Babylon the great is fallen, is fallen, and is become the habitation of devils, and the hold of every foul spirit, and a cage of every unclean and hateful bird. (Revelation 18:1-2)

Daniel in Babylon cried out to God! "As it is written in the law of Moses, all this evil is come upon us: yet made we not our prayer before the LORD our God, **that we might turn from our iniquities, and understand thy truth.** Therefore hath the LORD watched upon the evil, and **brought it upon us: for the LORD our God is righteous in all his works which he doeth: for we obeyed not his voice.** And now, O Lord our God, that hast brought thy people forth out of the land of Egypt with a mighty hand, and hast gotten thee renown, as at this day; we have sinned, we have done wickedly. O Lord, according to all thy righteousness, I beseech thee, let thine anger and thy fury be turned away from thy city Jerusalem, thy holy mountain: because for our sins, and for the iniquities of our fathers, Jerusalem and thy people are become a reproach to all that are about us. Now therefore, O our God, hear the prayer of thy servant, and his supplications, and cause thy face to shine upon thy sanctuary that is desolate, for the Lord's sake. O my God, incline thine ear, and hear; open thine eyes, **and behold our desolations, and the city which is called by thy name: for we do not present our supplications before thee for our righteousnesses, but for thy great mercies."**

Daniel 12 is open. Michael is the mighty angel in Revelation 18, the same angel who led the Children of Israel out of Egypt, the same angel who was reincarnated as Jesus Christ our Lord and Saviour.

WHILE IN BABYLON THE JEWS REMEMBERED JERUSALEM THE PLACE OF THE SKULL

Jerusalem they remembered as the city where justice was meted out, where they lived in freedom as One Nation under God with liberty and justice for all. It is called today the undivided city where justice is for all Jews, Gentiles, Christians and Muslims

The Jews hide the Hill of Golgotha behind the bus station. To the left is the empty Garden Tomb. In the distance you hear the call to prayer from the Mosque. The call from everywhere to prayer turns our hearts toward God. Death was forever conquered in Jerusalem, at the Place of the Skull Jesus conquered Lucifer!

An amazing gift of love has been found in a little cross made from the bloody cross of Jesus. It is kept in a vault under the protection of the Armenian Priests in the Holy Sepulcher in Jerusalem. The dry blood is that of an alien when placed in water, it comes alive. The blood of Jesus has twenty four chromosomes. The blood of Mary with twenty three chromosomes needed the Y chromosome of the Father to make Jesus Christ his son.

We have twenty three chromosomes from our father and mother giving us humans forty six chromosomes. When one chromosome duplicates and a baby is born with forty seven chromosomes, you have a Downs Syndrome child. It is beyond our comprehension for someone to survive with only twenty four chromosomes. It is comparable for us to trying to explain *infinity.*

You can test the DNA of a Pharaoh, but it takes living blood to test for chromosomes. Orthodox Jews have had time to test and research this blood since 1982? You see God has given the Jews a second chance to figure out they killed Jesus our Messiah! It is said when the blood of Jesus was injected into man it caused intense mental anguish to see human suffering. Volunteers wanted to die.

Ron Wyatt, a Christian Seventh Day Sabbath keeper found the cave and the Ark of the Covenant as an amateur archeologist. The Rabbis will tell you, they have the blood of the Lamb of God with twenty four chromosomes of our Messiah. They know Ron Wyatt. They know the name of the four angels guarding the Law of God's Government. No Jewish Priest has been able to come into the presence of God, boldly unto the Throne of Grace. Ron Wyatt had to pull them out of the tunnel leading into the cave.

Ron Wyatt is an affront to Jews, Muslims and some Christians. He did his best to obey the Ten Commandments. He had the gift of the Holy Ghost with respect and dignity to our Creator. His humility was in knowing he needed the Robe of Christ's Righteousness because our righteousness is like filthy rags. Ron was perfected in accepting his salvation through the blood the Lamb. Humility humbles pride.

"Then Peter said unto them, Repent, and be baptized every one of you in the name of Jesus Christ for the remission of sins, and ye shall receive the gift of the Holy Ghost." (Act 2:38).

During the Holocaust, no *one like the Son of God was with those placed in the fiery furnaces* of Auschwitz. The Jews have been given a second chance. Those who said, "His blood be upon our heads and the heads of our children's children," made a prayer God answered.

Christians are finding their Messiah is Jesus an innocent Jew. Before Jesus died, Shadrach, Meshach and Abednego had the Holy Spirit of God and one like the Son of God walked with them in the fiery furnace in Babylon. **But Jesus had to die at the hands of his family and friends! It was prophesied. God is giving the Jews a second chance**. We want to be found sinless when Jesus comes.

Will we like Mel Gibson use Jesus as the scapegoat for our sins crucifying the son of God again? Will we turn to obedience rather than sacrifice? We are not saved by keeping the Ten Commandments like the Jews did. "In as much as ye have done unto the least of these my brethren ye have done it unto me." Defend Jesus the Jew!

Christians are saved by faith in the blood of the Lamb. Jews on the other hand are like Doubting Thomas, they needed tangible proof their ancestors killed an innocent Jew, their Messiah. There is a growth of Christian Jews and Christians studying their roots in Judaism. They are caught with blood of Jesus on their hands. But before we judge the Jews, have we become so calloused we would say, "Let his blood be upon our children and their children?" Let the death of Jesus be placed on the head of Jesus because we want to continue in sin against God and His Government?

The forerunner of Christ is the message of Elijah and John the Baptist. Elijah felt he was the only one left among those loyal to God. John the Baptist came to humble the leadership who feared Jesus and God would take away their Kingdom. John the Baptist uttered the word of truth. "You should not be sleeping with your brother's wife." The sexual immorality of King Herod was minor compared to who he murdered to obtain his throne. Earthly men who fear losing *their throne* are so power hungry they would destroy their own. Immorality is the opposite of Immortality which is eternal life, the ability to live forever under Gods Government. Immorality is the immoral quality, character, or conduct; wickedness; evilness reflected in open sin against God. She the false church is called *the whore*. "And the ten horns which thou sawest upon the beast, these shall hate the whore, and shall make her desolate and naked, and shall eat her flesh, and burn her with fire." (Revelation 17:16). She uses Jesus Christ as the fall guy. She says, "Go ahead and sin" crucify Jesus again. Without the Law of God we would not know what sin against God and man is.

CHAPTER ONE includes the reason God hid the meaning in His symbols. One day the World would want to know if there is life in space. And if there is life, it is friendly or evil? Is there a Creator who can *create a law* that offers His son as the ultimate sacrifice for sin? When sin was found in Heaven, it was found in a living robot, made to live eternally, that went over to the over side, like Darth Vader.

The concept of sin would be played out in the relationship of father to his son. To understand evil is to feel the pain and estrangement from those we love. To understand joy that causes us to cry, is the uniting with those who also love us, just the way we are.

And when we get to know our son, we do not want our son to die, at our own hands, for our sin! Abraham was faced with a choice. Obey God and *sacrifice his son, for his sin.* But God does not want *any man take the sin, for what Lucifer has suggested to us.* In Sarah providing a human solution to Gods promise to give her a baby she provided Abraham with an excuse to have sexual intercourse with the maid.

Abraham might have thought twice if he knew God could make his barren wife, have a child. And who would think God could do this thing? Maybe God would provide an heir through the maid.

Standing over his son, with a knife, I wonder how Isaac was so compliant to be tied down and obey his father? Isaac must have loved his father very much. Or Isaac might have wanted to die, rather than live in the conflict between his mother and Hagar? Whatever the reason Isaac obeyed, will be a mystery. But God used the supernatural to show He was the Creator. How could an old man and woman have a child? What was the maid to do without the inheritance her son would not now receive? Was she to be cursed? No, she was to be blessed, and become a mighty nation and Ismael would have twelve sons of his own.

God did provide a "ram, a male lamb." God would provide his own son, His Lamb, as the sacrifice for sin. Because Lucifer was to be given a chance to prove his ability to be the Creator and sit on Gods Throne. But earth would be the living sacrifice of life and death, death and life.

God and his son Michael made the plan of salvation before the world began. And yes, the Universe would have to see where jealousy would lead. Many have wanted the power to rule the world. If the world could understand the *love of the father for his son,* they could understand <u>the father would rather die himself, than watch his son die!</u>

Ishmael would go free. He would not be the sacrifice for Abraham's sin of going to the maid. God said, Sarah would be the wife of the baby that would come. Only one son could carry the seed that would go to make the Temple Mount a place of prayer for all nations! By adoption we become the Sons and Daughters of God.

It was necessary by law, that the world should be warned with signs and wonders. The supernatural God would show up, where men would allow God to reveal himself, by setting themselves apart, to let God use them. Blood Moon what a lovely sight last night!

If the devil knew the Heavenly Courts decision would go in favor of Jesus Christ, he would excite the Nations to destroy the world. Because once the power of God is revealed in man to stand up and say, "I'm saved by the blood of the Lamb." The devil is made.

Lucifer knew the penalty for murdering the Son of God. If Lucifer didn't get attention, he would get it by undermining the Government of God. Lucifer would prefer bad attention, rather than no attention. He was jealous of Michael the Archangel in Heaven.

Heavenly beings were innocent in listening to the advice of Lucifer. Maybe God could give special privileges to his angels. After all, what good is it to obey God, if you can't have something special for obedience? If Lucifer would rule the Universe, he would have special treatment for those who ruled under him. Preferential treatment would be due the king.

History has enacted this plan of the kings and queens to receive special notoriety! The French Revolution was the masses against the King of France. And the rebellion against civil authority berthed a new rebel against God and the universal catholic church with men who called themselves atheists. What good is a God who gives us freedom of conscience then forces us to live within a church who causes us to feel like slaves to their dogmas?

What good is a God who gives us freedom and liberty who withholds justice? Why must innocent people be the benevolent fall guy? Why must we suffer for the sins of others? When in doubt blame Connie! Blame someone including God, for he put the snake in the tree didn't he! He told us to learn good and evil. We would judge the angels, Michael or Lucifer. What more could want, than freedom from Lucifer the voice we hear making suggestions of how we can achieve happiness! Think about that! Happiness as a goal?

Chapter II

The First Angel Sounds

"The first angel sounded, [his trumpet] and there followed **hail and fire mingled with blood,** and they were cast upon the earth: and the **third part of trees** was burnt up, and **all green grass** was burnt up (Revelation 8:7).

NO! God has no war against his grass or trees. He does not destroy! "But they rebelled, and vexed his holy Spirit: therefore he was turned to be their enemy, *and* he fought against them." (Isaiah 63:10) He just stops protecting us. We didn't appreciate what all he was doing to protect us!

Pharisees like trees with leaves but no figs Jesus cursed. Hypocrites have no fruit of the Spirit. Pride is their enemy. Those who feel they are closest to God *by their position or blood line may compare their position and blood with Jesus the head of his church.*

The first trumpet reveals judgment on religious men like grass with no roots going down into the water of life. Trees like men who produce pride instead of the fruit of the Holy Spirit. Hail represents judgment, against those who deny God and his son. Fire refines character, like the assayer of metal, who invites us to remove sin from our lives before he comes. We embrace his righteousness. We see ourselves as sinners in the face of his perfect life. "I am not God" is our plea in all humility!

Pride was the downfall of the arrogant King of Babylon. He boasted of his great achievements giving the glory to himself. God allowed King Nebuchadnezzar, a gift of seven years of insanity. All it took was for King Nebuchadnezzar to say was "Look what I have done!" Pride? You want to compare yourself with God?

"*The tree* that thou sawest, which grew, and was strong, whose height reached unto the heaven, and the sight thereof to all the earth; Whose leaves *were* fair, and the fruit thereof much, and in it *was* meat for all; under which the beasts of the field dwelt, and upon whose branches the fowls of the heaven had their habitation: ***It is thou, O king,*** that art grown and become strong: for thy greatness is grown, and reacheth unto heaven, and thy dominion to the end of the earth. And whereas the king saw a watcher and an holy one coming down from heaven, and saying, Hew the tree down, and destroy it; yet leave the stump of the roots thereof in the earth, even with a band of iron and brass, in the tender grass of the field; and let it be wet with the dew of heaven, and *let* his portion *be* with the beasts of the field, till seven times pass over him; This *is* the interpretation, O king, and this *is* the decree of the most High, which is come upon my lord the king." (Daniel 4:20 -24 emphasis added)

God was crowned King of the first Kingdom of Gold just as prophecy foretold. Babylon was One Nation under God invisible with liberty and justice for all. And the King of Babylon gave God permission to take the glory *after he lived like a beast for seven years.*

"When the wicked spring as the grass, and when all the workers of iniquity do flourish; *it is* that they shall be destroyed forever." (Psalms 92:7 emphasis added).

"Let no man deceive you by any means: for *that day shall not come,* except there come a falling away first, and that man of sin be revealed, the son of perdition; Who opposeth and exalteth himself above all that is called God, or that is worshipped; so that he as God sitteth in the temple of God, shewing himself that he is God. (2 Thessalonians 2:3, 4 emphasis added).

Who dare sit in Gods House, thinking to change the times and laws of God? (Daniel 7:25) Because he waits on his Red Horse it seems evil has gotten worse. Does no one consult God? That is why he left the first temple. No one wanted his opinion. So, the Holy Shekinah Glory, paused as he left, and no one missed him. So he left. And the downfall of Jerusalem attests to a God who is dismissed, walks away. And we have our wish, for Lucifer to take over. How does that look? Got any good ideas on how to make over the world?

CHAPTER III

THE SECOND ANGEL SOUNDS
THE CURSE OF GODS WRATH
BEGAN ON SEPTEMBER 11, 2001

"And the second angel sounded,[a trumpet warning of destruction judgments] and as it were a great mountain burning with fire was cast into the sea: and the third part of the sea became blood" (Revelation 8:8 emphasis added).

What you are about to see is God revealing He is the master mind behind all prophecy. The wrath of God is in the Old Testament. Jonathan Cahn shows how God has led in the past, to warn the world of the death of the wicked. Pride and arrogancy of man, in thinking he can sit on God's Throne and play God is over.

Symbols in the earthly Temple, pointed to the day when Jesus the Lamb of God would be the blood sacrifice for all the sins beginning with Adam and Eve. The perfect light of Jesus the seven fold candlestick brings back the Holy Spirit to the hearts of mankind. Make us a sanctuary, the perfect light to shine in spiritual darkness! God is revealing the Truth about our arch enemy Lucifer, whose name is The Destroyer Reveltion 9:11. A created being wants to be worshipped like God and have all people on earth bow down to him, is the goal of Lucifer the AntiChrist.

"Know ye not that we shall judge angels? how much more things that pertain to this life?" (I Corinthians 6:2-3).

Freedom allows you to judge the angels Michael the Archangel! Lucifer, The Destroyer, is unmasked. Two angels you shall judge. We like Adam and Eve have learned from cause and effect how Lucifer tempts us to destroy. Jesus Christ our angel, our messenger and best friend opens our eyes to the Great Controversy between between Michael and Lucifer! Vote for your Messiah.

THE SACRED MOUNTAIN KINGDOM

"You said in your heart, I will ascend to heaven; I will raise my throne above the stars of God; I will sit enthroned on the mount of assembly, on the utmost heights of the sacred mountain." (Isaiah 14:13).

MOUNTAIN EQUALS KINGDOM

Lucifer wanted to be worshipped. He was given rulership over Earth. Lucifer challenged the Government of God. Michael the son of God entered into God's tent and they make their game plan. Lucifer was jealous he could not be included in the plan of salvation! Jesus would be the scapegoat, until it was time for Lucifer to exposed! Jesus our Bridegroom is on the way to earth, like the dark cloud over Mount Sinai.

Michael the winner has taken rulership of the Earth. The stakes are high! God would play by His Rules. No guns of course. God would use the sword of truth. Lucifer would use every advantage to get men to bow down to him including force, terror, and deception.

We set up an imaginary heaven, no lice, no flies, no grumbling, no different ideas how to run the church or group…sounds like Heaven to me.

"And all the people saw the thundering's, and the lightning's, and the noise of the trumpet, and the mountain smoking: and when the people saw it, they removed, and stood afar off. And they said unto Moses, Speak thou with us, and we will hear: but let not God speak with us, lest we die. And Moses said unto the people, *Fear not: for God is come to prove you, and that his fear may be before your faces, that ye sin not"* (Exodus 20:18–20 emphasis added).

God laid down the law for His House. He keeps the Law. Lucifer on the other hand, has a plan to take over the Kingdom of God. And when he can't get his way Lucifer's destroys like a spoiled child. God is not on Lucifer's side!

"And I will render unto Babylon and to all the inhabitants of Chaldea all their evil that they have done in Zion in your sight, saith the LORD. *Behold, I am against thee, <u>O destroying mountain,</u> saith the LORD, which destroyest all the earth: and I will stretch out mine hand upon thee, and roll thee down from the rocks, and will make thee a burnt mountain"* (Jeremiah 51:24 emphasis added).

God is revealing himself! Lucifer is exposed as The Destroyer of good relationship in family, church, and friends!

ABLAZE!

"Then Nebuchadnezzar the king was astonished, and rose up in haste, *and* spake, and said unto his counselors, Did not we cast three men bound into the midst of the fire? They answered and said unto the king, True, O king. He answered and said, Lo, I see four men loose, walking in the midst of the fire, and they have no hurt; and the form of the fourth is like the Son of God. Then Nebuchadnezzar came near to the mouth of the burning fiery furnace, *and* spake, and said, Shadrach, Meshach, and Abednego, *ye servants of the most high God,* come forth, and come *hither.* Then Shadrach, Meshach, and Abednego, came forth of the midst of the fire. (Daniel 3:24–26).

"And it shall come to pass in the last days, saith God, *I will pour out of my Spirit upon all flesh*: and your sons and your daughters shall prophesy, and your young men shall see visions, and your old men shall dream dreams" (Acts 2:17). They receive the Holy Spirit accept the power and do not deny the Holy Spirit! The coals of fire are for all flesh.

"Then one of the seraphim [angel] flew to me with *a live coal in his hands*, which he had taken with tongs from the altar. With it he touched my mouth and said, 'See this has touched your lips, *your guilt is taken away and your sin atoned for."* (Isaiah 6:6-7) God is revealing himself. Now he is a God of wrath, but still zealous for truth to out. There is a surprise ending. It is as if he really is a Mother Hen wanting to protect and defend all men **who call on him.**

Ablaze
is defined
as *fire* or *eager.*
We can say God is
an all - consuming *fire*
he can destroy sin forever and
he is eager to have us understand
why he must destroy Satan and his
angels. Ablaze is the very nature
of God who passionately wants
to prove to us he is our friend
and allied with us to fight
the war against Lucifer.
The fiery furnace did
not kill the
three
Hebrew
slaves
from
Jerusalem.
Instead
the king
saw four
men
walking
in the fire!
The fourth
looked
like
a Son
of the
God.
At Pentecost,
the disciples of Jesus
seemed to have *tongues of fire.*

Waters Symbolize Seas Of Prople

"And he saith unto me, The waters which thou sawest, where the whore sitteth, are peoples, and multitudes, and nations, and tongues."(Revelation 17:15).

Water and dry land may be the most unique words used as Bible symbols. It is as if God looks down on earth, as a fishbowl. The oceans are where the fish or sea creatures live, and swim in schools. Dry land or earth, appears, and has very few people.

"And I beheld another beast coming up out of the earth; and he had two horns like a lamb, and he spake as a dragon." (Revelation 13:11). USA begins in prophecy like a buffalo calf. This beast or Kingdom will one day speak like a dragon. "And he causeth all, both small and great, rich and poor, free and bond, to receive a mark in their right hand, or in their foreheads: And that no man might buy or sell, save he that had the mark, or the name of the beast, or the number of his name. (Revelation 13:16-17).

GODS POINT OF VIEW

In a sea, a sea of humanity, like a chrysalis, we can
be wrapped up in ourselves. However, in waiting
we have the Bible that interprets itself!
A sea of people is a definite revelation
from God, using a word for a special
meaning that only the Bible can supply!
Our planet is made up of dry land and water.
From God's point of view, we are like a fishbowl.
He looks down at us like a sea of people! He sees us
traveling like schools of fish. Dry land is an area not
densely populated. Rural areas have more cows than humans.
However, many of God's riddles have to do with nature.
If we lose our saltiness, our joy, we have nothing to add
to life. Seasoned Christians, bring a blessing in living.
Their wit and humor delights us with their uncommon
way of seeing life through a filter that gives them
wings to think of a better way to catch a fish,
or mow a lawn. Jesus taught us to be fishers
of men! Fish, crabs, and sea creatures
cannot glorify God! But people can!
Where do you find a sea of people? God describes waters like a
huge city, with apartments, many languages, cultures, foods, and
religions living together. Ideas are exchanged on a daily basis.
New York City might be compared to the tower of Babel.
Sea ports are known for their ruckus controversies.
Why would God recommend country living?
The word tower in Hebrew means
Assayer of metal. Are we made
of sand and clay or have we
characters of gold?

ONE THIRD!
LUCIFER DECEIVED OF THE ANGELS

1/3

"His tail [Lucifer] swept a third of the stars out of the sky and flung them to the earth" (Revelation 12:4).

We learned stars are angels in (Revelation 1:20) But these are evil *angels* supernatural created beings who are not your friends. They are Gods enemies bent on destroying you and all nations!

When John the Baptist found himself in prison for saying, "You should not be living with your brother's wife," he said, "He [Jesus] must increase, but I must decrease." (John 3:30). John the Baptist might worry for his head in our generation. Past prophecy shows dual applications to truth and applies to anyone preparing the way for the Lord to come. Blessed are they that mourn!

"The voice of him that crieth in the wilderness, Prepare ye the way of the LORD, make straight in the desert a highway for our God. Every valley shall be exalted, and every mountain and hill shall be made low: and the crooked shall be made straight, and the rough places plain: **And the glory of the LORD shall be revealed, and all flesh shall see *it* together: for the mouth of the LORD hath spoken *it*.** The voice said, Cry. And he said, What shall I cry? All flesh *is* grass, and all the goodliness thereof *is* as the flower of the field: The grass withereth, the flower fadeth: because the spirit of the LORD bloweth upon it: surely the people *is* grass. The grass withereth, the flower fadeth: but the word of our God shall stand for ever. (Isaiah 40:3-8).

God is not sending an idle warning! Praise the Lord he cares! He keeps his word. He is revealing himself. By himself.

RED BLOOD A TOKEN

"And the blood shall be to you for a token upon the houses where ye are: and **when I see the blood, I will pass over you**, and the plague shall not be upon you to destroy you, when I smite the land of Egypt" (Exodus 12:13).

"The blood of goats and bulls and the ashes of a heifer sprinkled on those who are ceremonially unclean sanctify them so that they are outwardly clean. How much more, then, will the blood of Christ, who *through the eternal Spirit* offered himself unblemished to God, cleanse our consciences from acts that lead to death, so that we may serve the living God!" (Hebrews 9:14).

"Imagine finding the literal blood of Jesus, with twenty four chromosomes of living blood that purchased our freedom to worship God, with liberty and justice for all? Freedom is not free. The blood of Jesus purchased your freedom when Jesus voluntarily gave his life, in a blood sacrifice.

Ask a Rabbi! What will you do with the blood of our Messiah with twenty four chromosomes? Will you defend His Kingdom of Truth too?

"Thou hast loved righteousness, and hated iniquity; therefore God, *even* thy God, hath anointed thee with the oil of gladness above thy fellows. (Hebrews 1:9).

The color red, suggests to some it means death. To a Christian death is conquered, and red is happiness! With this joy and appreciation we can be thankful for all Jesus has done for us.

CREATUES IN THE SEA

"Come follow me and I will make you fishers of men" (Matthew 4:19). You are the bait. God sends *fish* to you. There is a joke. A man goes into a restaurant. He asks the waiter, "Do you serve crabs?" The waiter answers, "We serve anyone, sir."

Do we serve everyone who enters the House of God with dignity? Can God send us clown fish and angel fish?

Wherever you find a sea of people—from *sharks, angel fish* to *octopi*—they are all game for the fisherman Jesus can train. Sometimes you may feel like the bait. They may come to you but it is Jesus who reels them in. Evangelism is the purest form of watching God work. Jesus will show up to reveal his love, healing and power if we give him the glory! Even false healers can invite God to heal a soul that he has blessed and God will grant the request.

I've seen Romanian Orthodox Priest threaten: "If they own a Bible, study a Bible or translate the Bible, I will not do their funeral or the funeral of their friend." They are told, they will not go to heaven they will die in hell. They will not talk to anyone but the priest. They say, "Do you want me to die?"

No organization goes into heaven. No sin can enter heaven. God could not watch his son die if he could change his laws! He turned his head in awful silence. The silence of God right now, watching us make a decision to continue in sin separates us from him! That is why God hates sin!

SHIPWRECKS

"Timothy, my son, I give you this instruction in keeping with the prophecies once made about you, so that by following them you may fight the good fight, holding on to faith and a good conscience. Some have rejected these and so have shipwrecked their faith" (Timothy 1:18–19).

Timothy was guided by his mother and grandmother. Timothy was seen as child of promise who would fight the good fight of faith and bring many to Jesus. Timothy seemed to be predestined to be a teacher to watch God work his miracles.

And in preparing Timothy for the suffering and pain he would encounter, his mother reminded her son, to not make shipwreck of his faith.

Do not make shipwreck of your faith when man says you cannot buy or sell! You trust in God. (Revelation 13).

Our Ship Carries Us And All We Own: On The Sea Of Life

All our baggage furniture, photos, pets, are *on our ship*. When we face losing pets, family, friends, bank accounts, will we make shipwreck of our faith?

This is becoming a reality with prices rising. We are looking into the unknown. Is Heaven really a safe place? In heaven can we jump off a mountain and fly? Would you like to stay in this atmosphere all your life? What possibilities are within our reach that we can truly hold in this life and the next?

When we feel anxious *our ship* might sink, we have Peter to thank. Peter got out of his comfort zone keeping his eyes on Jesus. And if we try to trust in our self we sink into mental, social, physical and spiritual depression. Faith is an experience with Jesus.

The Holy Spirit calls us! I get called quite often! I call it the Holy Spirit attack! The remedy is to get up and read my Bible. I place a date in my Bible when God answers a question I can't put into words? By taking time out with my Bible, I always learn something new that enlightens my heart and makes me smile. I have felt my muscles literally relax. That's a good feeling!

" For I earnestly protested unto your fathers in the day *that* I brought them up out of the land of Egypt, *even* unto this day, rising early and protesting, saying, Obey my voice. Yet they obeyed not, nor inclined their ear, but walked everyone in the imagination of their evil heart: therefore I will bring upon them all the words of this covenant, which I commanded *them* to do; but they did *them* not. (**Jeremiah 11:6-7**).

Elvis Presley sang, "Why don't we call him, before we lose our way? Sometimes we have to go astray to find our way back home to Jesus. We have to feel the pain of loss, to know we want someone better. No one compares with Jesus!

If your boat is stuck on a sand bar and you think there is no way out, that is a lie. When you get to the end of your rope, there is a hand ready to carry you. When you call on the name of the Lord, he will save you! (Romans 10:13) Today is good time call on Jesus to see what he has done for you. He never stops listening.

REVIEW:

Throw something like a *mountain on fire* into a *sea of humanity.* That mountain on fire is ablaze to reassure us God's Kingdom is in control. He knew this would happen. Those who have denied his Holy Spirit will continue in denial. One third of the perfect heavenly angels were deceived. The blood of the Lamb brings a free gift of salvation and ratifies the Government of God. We can be right with God and man. Yes, some fish die, but these are not fish, they are real people, jumping from skyscrapers. Yes those who placed their confidence in things need to beware. A shipwreck makes us aware of our need for Jesus. The devil is delighted when you blame God for what he has destroyed. Why else would Lucifer destroy? Fact is the devil is behind all destruction, war and division.

Those who placed their confidence in the blood of the Lamb pray for God to vindicate them and end this controversy. By repentance we turn away from evil. We continue to face the devil behind each crisis. We call on God to help us find the right path to a spiritual resolution by trusting in Him not man. Faith builder he is.

Gods provides for burros and goats in the desert. He can provide water in dry land, just as he did when the children were in the wilderness. He provides our bread and water. Our angels go ahead of us, to prepare the way, for us to grow smarter, and wiser. They take us to where we need to go. Jesus learned the same way. He suffered. For some of us we learn by cause and effect.

I taught seven preteen youth the meaning of these symbols. They all drew a picture of 9-11-2001 in New York City. I was told I could no longer teach Bible Symbols. I was teaching the Bible.

Jonathan Cahn had not yet written his book The Harbinger of 9-11-2001. What a relief to my soul! The Koran has 9-11-2001 in it too, I understand. God becoming our enemy is not new, staying our enemy, leaves us something to do! He has time on his side! He can wait another forty years as we wander around on earth! Can't promise you your shoes will not wear out. Would someone please ask God to end this war on his Kingdom? Yes, I am talking to you! A prayer will be heard, that calls on God, to end Lucifer's destructive bent! Too many are welcoming his addicting games.

DO NOT MAKE SHIPWRECK OF YOUR FAITH!

"And the second angel sounded, and as it were a great mountain burning with fire was cast into the sea: and the third part of the sea became blood; And the third part of the creatures which were in the sea, and had life, died; and the third part of the ships were destroyed." (Revelation 8:8-9).

Enter The Voice Of Dead Prophets

I cannot take credit for translating these symbols. C. Mervyn Maxwell translated the Second Trumpet of Revelation 8:8, 9 before his death in 1970. He wrote, "Image a Third World army invading Washington [D.C.] setting fire to the Pentagon and White House." IN GODS CARES II.

Rarely do you find a one sentence paragraph but Maxwell seemed to write this in a moment of trying to help us understand the fall of the Roman Empire. Generally it believed to be at the hands of sailors coming out of Carthage on North Africa, attacking cities along the Mediterranean. They were called Vandals

Renaissance and Early Modern writers characterized the Vandals as barbarians, "sacking and looting" Rome. This led to the use of the term *vandalism*, to describe any senseless destruction, particularly the *barbarian* defacing of artworks. However, modern historians tend to regard the Vandals during the transitional period (from Late Antiquity to the Early Middle Ages) as perpetuators, not destroyers, of Roman culture. (Wikipedia)

I laughed to read, *the vandals* helped perpetuate the Roman culture? I sigh. The name *terrorist* has replaced *vandalism*. History is repeating. A hand full men guided by the mysterious Lucifer sought revenge.

However, Ellen White and Mervyn Maxwell are vindicated by the terrorist attack on the Twin Towers on 9-11-2001. God knew buildings would be built, higher and higher! "No earthly power can stay the hand of God. No material can be used in the erection of buildings that will preserve them from destruction when God's appointed time comes to send retribution of men for their disregard of His law and for their selfish ambition." Volume 9, *Testimonies to the Church*. Lucifer is behind all destruction and rebellion against God!

"And the dragon was wroth with the woman, and went to make war with the remnant of her seed, which keep the commandments of God, and have the testimony of Jesus Christ." (Revelation 12:17). The testimony of Jesus I like is, "Neither do I condemn thee, go and sin no more." (John 8:11).

Chapter IV

Comfort Ye My People Walter's Story

My door swung open, and my son came in, asking, "What happens after 9/11?" He had not unpacked his truck or his clothes from college.

My mind ran along the lines of, *Who cares what happens after 9-11?* I pointed him to our library and a book of prophecy written over a hundred years ago:

Walter, whose nickname is "911," settled into a chair and began to read aloud, starting on page 11.

"On one occasion when in New York City, I was in the night season called upon to behold buildings rising story after story towards heaven. These buildings were warranted to be fireproof, and they were erected to glorify their owners and builders. Higher and still higher these buildings rose. In them the most costly material was used. Those to whom these buildings belonged were not asking themselves: "How can we best glorify God?" The Lord was not in their thoughts.

"I thought: "Oh, that those who are thus investing their means could see their course as God sees it! They are piling up magnificent buildings, but how foolish in the sight of the Ruler of the Universe is their planning and devising. *They are not studying with all the powers of heart and mind how they may glorify God. They have lost sight of this, the first duty of man.*"

"As these lofty buildings went up, the owners rejoiced with ambitious *pride* that they had money to use in gratifying self and *provoking the envy of their neighbors.* Much *money that they thus invested had been obtained through exaction, through grinding down the poor.* They forgot that in heaven an account of every business transaction is kept; every unjust deal, every fraudulent act, is there recorded. The time is coming when in their fraud and insolence *men will reach a point that the Lord will not permit them to pass,* and they will learn that there is a limit to the forbearance of Jehovah.

"The scene that next passed before me was an alarm of fire. Men looked at the lofty and supposedly fire-proof buildings and said: "They are perfectly safe." *But these buildings were consumed as if made of pitch.* The fire engines could do nothing to stay the destruction. The firemen were unable to operate the engines.

"I am instructed that when the Lord's time comes, should no change have taken place in the hearts of proud, ambitious human beings, men will find that the hand that had been strong to save will be strong to destroy. No earthly power can stay the hand of God. No material can be used in the erection of buildings that will preserve them from destruction when God's appointed time comes to send retribution on men for their disregard of His law and for their selfish ambition." *Testimonies to the Church, Volume 9,* by Ellen G. White, beginning on page 11.

Walter was reading aloud, making me his captive audience. I listened to show respect for his interest in prophecy. However, there was a *progression* as he read—one I had heard before.

I walked to my desk, picked up a book called GOD CARES II. Revelation 8:8-9 was translated using symbols, just as we have done. "Imagine a third world army invading Washington D.C. and setting fire to the Pentagon and White House." (C. Mervyn Maxwell, *God Cares II*). This prophecy takes us back to the Bible. Mervyn Maxwell died before he knew he was inspired by the Holy Spirit.

Spring break in 2002 was over. But why had Walter asked me, "What happens after 9-11?" His nickname is 911! Is Walter the only one who cares what happens after 9-11-2001? That night two prophecies came together.

Thirteen years after 9-11-2001 I find myself very much alone and writing this book. I find myself defending dead prophets including

Jesus. I now know GOD cares! He sends Michael to stand up to vindicate his prophets and saints.

"Rejoice over her, *thou* heaven, and *ye* holy apostles and prophets; for God hath avenged you on her. (Revelation 18:20).

"And in her was found the blood of prophets, and of saints, and of all that were slain upon the earth. (Revelation 18:24).

CHAPTER V

THE THIRD ANGEL SOUNDED BEWARE OF ENVY AND BITTERNESS!

"And the third angel sounded, and there *fell a great star from heaven, burning as it were a lamp*, and it fell upon the third part of the rivers, and upon the fountains of waters; And the name of the star is called Wormwood: and the third part of the waters became wormwood; and many men died of the waters, because they were made bitter" (Revelation 8:10–11).

Invidia, <u>allegorical</u> painting by <u>Giotto di Bondone</u>, ca. 1305-1306 Wikipedia

Giotto di Bondone captured the hidden spiritual meaning of a women standing with her feet in hell, her tongue, like a snake comes back to bite her. She grasps her bag of money. Her words are poison.

Allegories convey an immense power to illustrate complex ideas and concepts in ways that are easily digestible and tangible to its viewers, readers, or listeners. However a man dressed in red pajamas with horns and pitch fork, fails to define the envy Lucifer has for

Jesus and is followers. Lucifer's bitterness drives to divide and destroy everything and everyone who loves Jesus.

Stars = are holy angels, messengers, protectors; however this angel has a name that describes unholy.

Wormwood = by definition is a plant that tastes very bitter. *Bitters* added to drinks may disguise its true nature.

A fallen star = is false messenger, like a fallen angel, like Lucifer, who is a false messenger of God.

"And ye have seen their abominations, and their idols, wood and stone, silver and gold, which *were* among them: Lest there should be among you man, or woman, or family, or tribe, *whose heart turneth away this day from the LORD our God, to go and serve the gods* of these nations; lest there should be among you a root that beareth gall and wormwood; And it come to pass, when he heareth the words of this curse, that he bless himself in his heart, saying, I shall have peace, though I walk in the imagination of mine heart, to add drunkenness to thirst: The LORD will not spare him, but then the anger of the LORD and his jealousy shall smoke against that man, and all the curses that are written in this book shall lie upon him, and the LORD shall blot out his name from under heaven. (Deuteronomy 29:17-20).

"And the great dragon was cast out, that old serpent, called the Devil, and Satan, which deceiveth the whole world: he was cast out into the earth, and his angels were cast out with him. And I heard a loud voice saying in heaven, *Now is come salvation, and strength, and the kingdom of our God, and the power of his Christ: for the accuser of our brethren is cast down, which accused them before our God day and night.*"

"And they overcame him *by the blood of the Lamb,* and *by the word of their testimony; and they loved not their lives unto the death.* Therefore rejoice, ye heavens, and ye that dwell in them. Woe to the inhabiters of the earth and of the sea! for the devil is come down unto you, having great wrath, because he knoweth that he hath but a short time." (Revelation 12:9-12).

TESTIMONY OF A TEENAGER:

A young teenager was troubled with demons. She got the idea she wanted a vampire in her attic. She found a young girl, who was demon possessed, they had a séance. Against the advice of the other girls she spoke to the demon. All summer she could not sleep at night. The demons made noise, talked, and moved her bed.

A minister was visiting from India. Trish wanted to talk to this pastor. He had seen people come out of being possessed by demons. We saw the film in India of this happening.

They sat down, he across from her, face to face. He looked at the black wrist bands, with the skull and crossbones on her arm, a trinket. He said, "In India, these are the ways they invite the devil into their lives."

Trish pulled eagerly to get the layers of black bands off her arm.

He said, "If you want to get rid of the demons, you will have to use the name of Jesus." He looked up and saw her willingness to learn.

She memorized these words, "I am saved by the blood of the lamb, Jesus Christ is my Saviour." That night she was no longer kept awake by spirits that talked, shook her bed, and deprived her of sleep.

If we resist the devil he will flee. If we discern the devil and meet him head on *we will have a testimony.* We will not be caught in bitterness and envy when the devil disrupts. We will not lose our peace of mind! We will say, "I will not change the times and law of God," God will defend me.

Like this minister, we will point others back to Jesus. "If we confess our sins he is faithful and just to forgive us from all unrighteousness. We are saved by the blood of the lamb and Jesus Christ is our Saviour." We have found the way to resist, the enemy.

Resistance is an army against lies about God and Jesus. God cares! Be ready to *see the good seed Jesus planted in every heart! Give a blessing to all,* who come in the name of Jesus, and in every heart he has planted a seed, that needs to be nourished with justice, mercy and humility. You be the sunshine, the joy, the person God made you to be, his servant.

Chapter VI

The Fourth Angel Sounds
Lucifer Brings Darkness

"And the fourth angel sounded, and the third part of the sun was smitten, and the third part of the moon, and the third part of the stars; so as the third part of them was darkened, and the day shone not for a third part of it, and the night likewise" (Revelation 8:12).

SIGNS IN THE SUN, MOON AND STARS

Sun of Righteousness is Jesus "But unto you that fear my name shall the *Sun* of righteousness arise with healing in his wings; and ye shall go forth, and grow up as calves of the stall." (Malachi 4:2).

Or are like the blood moon that shows we would rather crucify Jesus Christ for our sins than obey our Creator God. Don't forget the Holocaust when the Jews figured the death of one innocent man would place them without the Son of God, standing in the fiery furnaces with them.

Moon is Gods Church, His House. The *moon* reflects light from the "Sun of righteousness," like a church or individual who brings spiritual light into spiritual darkness. We reflect the light coming from the Son of God.

Stars are lights in darkness, like we are lights in spiritual darkness. "And there appeared a great wonder in heaven; a woman clothed with the sun, and the moon under her feet, and upon her head a crown of twelve stars:" (Revelation 12:1). The twelve *stars* on the head of the woman, is like a crown showing respect and dignity for the twelve disciples of Jesus.

One third = Again a reminder the devil wants to deceive and darken truth. The sun, moon, the stars obey God's will. The Son of God, the Church, and Bride are servants and disciples who desire to do his will.

Jesus told a story about a Bridegroom. While the bridegroom tarried, they all slumbered and slept. And at midnight there was a cry made, Behold, the bridegroom cometh; go ye out to meet him. Then all those virgins arose, and trimmed their lamps. And the foolish said unto the wise, Give us of your oil; for our lamps are gone out. But the wise answered, saying, Not so; lest there be not enough for us and you: but go ye rather to them that sell, and buy for yourselves. And while they went to buy, the bridegroom came; and they that were ready went in with him to the marriage: and the door was shut. (Matthew 25:6-10).

The Bridegroom is Jesus. He is the one who stands up to protect and defend his wife, the Bride, the Church.

"When I say unto the wicked, Thou shalt surely die; and thou givest him not warning, nor speakest to warn the wicked from his wicked way, to save his life; the same wicked man shall die in his iniquity; but his blood will I require at thine hand. Yet if thou warn the wicked, and he turn not from his wickedness, nor from his wicked way, he shall die in his iniquity; but thou hast delivered thy soul. Nevertheless if thou warn the righteous man, that the righteous sin not, and he doth not sin, he shall surely live, because he is warned; also thou hast delivered thy soul." (Ezekiel 3:18, 19, 21)

I resist the desire to let you slumber in peace, while you need the time and truth to WAKE UP! We have all gone to sleep. Wake up! The trumpets are sounding. Lift up the Trumpets and loud let them ring! Jesus is coming again! Cheer up ye children be joyful and sing, Jesus is coming again! Coming again! Coming Again, Jesus is coming again!

"For I will give you a mouth and wisdom, which all your adversaries shall not be able to gainsay nor resist." (Luke 21:15).

Mrs. White spoke to her angel, just like you can talk to your angel. She asked her angel to go tell a certain person about Jesus. The angel answered, "If they won't listen to the God of Mount Sinai, they won't listen to me."

Recently a new image appeared like a *Hand of God,* holding a crown. (Nasa.gov Hand of God image). God holding in his hand a crown of life! Something he wants to give all who have had to live in the lazar land of crazy things Lucifer has demanded, we do, see, feel, and touch!

There is beauty that remains from his perfectly created earth. The mountains speak of a Kingdom that reaches up to the sky. Keep your eyes on the rose, no thorns will grow in Heaven. See the sand in the oyster that grows into a pearl of great price. Jesus understood the pain of becoming worthy in your eyes, for sins he did not commit. His suffering identifies with our suffering.

Chapter VII

A Piercing Shrill Splits The Air Woe, Woe, Woe

"And I saw and I heard *one angel* flying in mid heaven, saying with a loud voice, **Woe! Woe! Woe! to the inhabitants of the earth,** *from the <u>rest of the voices</u> of the trumpet of the three angels being about to sound!*" (Revelation 8:13, emphasis added).

LISTEN TO THE CHANGE OF VOICES.

The all seeing eye of God'd Angel flys above the earth with a grand stand fly over.

"And I saw another angel fly in the midst of heaven, having the everlasting gospel to preach unto them that dwell on the earth, and to every nation, and kindred, and tongue, and people, Saying with a loud voice, *Fear God, and give glory to him; for the hour of his judgment is come: and worship him that made heaven, and earth, and the sea, and the fountains of waters.* And there followed another angel, saying, *Babylon is fallen, is fallen, that great city, because she made all nations drink of the wine of the wrath of her fornication.* And the third angel followed them, saying with a loud voice, *If any man worship the beast and his image, and receive his mark in his forehead, or in his hand, The same shall drink of the wine of the wrath of God, which is poured out without mixture into the cup of his indignation; and he shall be tormented with fire and brimstone in the presence of the holy angels, and in the presence of the Lamb:* And the smoke of their torment ascendeth up for ever and ever: and they have no rest day nor night, who worship the beast and his image, and whosoever receiveth the mark of his name. *Here is the patience of the saints: here are they that keep the commandments of God, and the faith of Jesus.* (Revelation 14:6-12)

"And he causeth all, both small and great, rich and poor, free and bond, to receive a mark in their right hand, or in their foreheads: And that no man might buy or sell, save he that had the mark, or the name of the beast, or the number of his name. (Revelation 13:16,17)

When God pours out his Holy Spirit on all flesh, it is the Holy Spirit, that gives us truth, to welcome a sound mind, to know good from evil! "And when he is come, he will reprove the world of sin, and of righteousness, and of judgment." (John 16:8).

God is exposing the false prophet, the false God, the false spirit while vindicating his true prophets, Himself, and the Holy Spirit.

There is a prophecy some church authorizes will say, "Take the mark on your right hand or forehead!" Your salvation depends on your love for Jesus and what He has done for you! "If you love me, keep my commandments." (John 14-15).

CHAPTER VIII

THE FIFTH ANGEL SOUNDED UNION OF CHURCH AND STATE AGAIN?

"And the fifth angel sounded, and I saw a star fall from heaven unto the earth: and to him was given the key of the bottomless pit. And he opened the bottomless pit; and there arose a smoke out of the pit, as the smoke of a great furnace; and the sun and the air were darkened by reason of the smoke of the pit. And there came out of the smoke locusts upon the earth: and unto them was given power, as the scorpions of the earth have power. *And it was commanded them that they should not hurt <u>the grass</u> of the earth, neither any <u>green thing</u>, neither any <u>tree;</u> but <u>only those men which have not the seal of God in their foreheads.</u>* (Revelation 9:1–5).

The blessing of the Lord is poured out on all flesh! The devil cannot hurt baby Christians, or anyone with life, or mature Christians but only those men who have chosen to not seal their faith firmly on the foundation of Jesus Christ and his forgiving love for all mankind.

ISLAM LIKE DICTATORSHIP IN PROPHECY

"Pliny, St. John's contemporary at the close of the first century, speaks of the Arabs as wearing the turban, having the hair long and uncut, with the mustache on the upper lip, or the beard, that 'venerable sign of manhood.'. As Gibbon, in Arab phraseology, call it . . .The Saracen policy was the wearing of the defensive armor. The breastplate of iron was a feature of description literally answering, like three others, to the Arab warriors to the sixth or seventh century." (*Horae Apocalyticae* Volume 1, 411-413.)

"Francisco Ribera (1537–1591), the renowned Jesuit commentator, assigned these two trumpets (along with all other trumpets) to a time still future to our day. Many Futurists see in the locusts a flight of demons not long before the second coming of Christ, swarming out of hell like bats out of the Carlsbad Caverns" (*God Cares II*, 244).

"The "Scorpion" Sting, The poison of the serpent or of the scorpion suggests a false religion. An early commentator, Joseph Mede, who wrote in the seventeenth century, declared that these Saracens were the first in history to set out for world conquest in the name of religion: "The tail, therefore, of a scorpion, with the sting, denotes the propagation of that diabolical false prophecy of Mohammed, with its whole apparatus, on which the Arabian locusts relying, not less than on warlike force, inflicted hurt, alas, wherever they went. Nay, this train of foulest errors, the Saracens first, from the creation of man, drew after them; and I believe no nation before them relying on a similar imposture in religion, and under the pretext of destroying the worship of idols, ever contended for the empire of the world" (*Clavis Apocalyptica* on Revelation 9).

Freedom of conscience is being threatened by church and state. Freedom purchased by the blood of the Lamb is being denied as the source of all true Freedom. Men are moving to threaten and force allegiance to man not God. Christ imparts power to resist the tyrant of temptation brought on by Lucifer. We need his Holy Spirit. Whoever hates sin instead of loving it, whoever resists and conquers those passions that have held sway within, displays the operation of a principle wholly from above. Jesus in me loves you!

CHAPTER IX

LUCIFER IS REVEALED AS THE DESTROYER

"And they had a king over them, which is the angel of the bottomless pit, whose name in the Hebrew tongue is Abaddon, but in the Greek tongue hath his name Apollyon" (Revelation 9:11). In English, *Apollyon* means "The Destroyer."

A man, 666, is The Destroyer in disguise. He is not quite God 777. He is at war with Gods character and government. He is the goat that got away every year on *the Day of Atonement*. On Gods Judgment Day, heaven voted for Jesus Christ to be no longer the sacrifice for sin. Lucifer is unmasked, he cannot hide. God is placing the blame of all sin on Lucifer!

If ever the devil is coming down to deceive the very elect, it is now. Those close to Christ Satan seeks to bring grief. Like Job we speak to God! We hear we are worthy of death for our sins. God on the other hand says, "Gird up your loins. Prepare to compare yourself with me?" And God points to those stars and wants to know if we can place just one in the sky?

WHAT DOES THIS MEAN TO YOU AND ISRAEL?

"This location[of the Ark of the Covenant] is recorded in our sources, and today, there are those who know exactly where this chamber is. And we know that the ark is still there, undisturbed, and waiting for the day when it will be revealed. An attempt was made some few years ago to excavate towards the direction of this chamber. This resulted in widespread Moslem unrest and rioting. They stand a <u>great deal</u> to lose if the Ark is revealed - for it will prove to the whole world that there really was a Holy Temple, and thus, that the Jews really do have a claim to the Temple Mount. (The official position of the Islamic Wakf, the body that governs over the Temple Mount, is that there never was a Holy Temple, and that the Jews have no rights whatsoever to the place)." (Temple Institute.org)

The Temple Institute confirms the Ark of the Covenant is found in Jerusalem. It can come out of hiding any day now. God has kept his covenant promise to all who follow Him. He can and will destroy The Destroyer and his angels! But not before his freedom is extended to all people.

The Orthodox Jews admit they have the blood of Our Messiah with twenty four chromosomes. Christians do not care if they have the physical evidence of an alien and stranger among us. Christians are saved by faith! Created in the image of God we are saved by the blood of the Lamb, Jesus Christ is our Saviour.

What will the Orthodox Jews do with Jesus? Will they deny again Jesus is the prophet, the prince, the king, the living Son of God, Our Messiah too?

Chapter X

The Sixth Angel Sounded Hear The Voices Of Power!

"And the sixth angel sounded, and I heard a voice from the *four horns of the golden altar* which is before God Saying to the sixth angel who had the trumpet, 'Loose the four angels who are bound in the great river Euphrates.' So the four angels who were ready for that hour, day, month, and year *were released to kill one-third of humanity*" (Revelation 9: 13–15 emphasis added)

Loose the four angels who have kept back the wrath of Lucifer! Remember that the angel from heaven said, *"Beware of the rest of the voices"* (Revelation 8:13 emphasis added).

The *horns of power in Heaven are represented by the horns of a bull. These mighty beasts, like a buffalo,* have power to encircle their baby calves. They lower their horns, to ward off predators to protect and defend their calf. The herd encircles the calf standing shoulder to shoulder giving an imposing stance.

You are seeing the horns of power lowering their heads to protect Jesus their little lamb, from being slaughtered by those who choose to openly disobey and pray for Jesus to die again for their sins. Jesus is no longer your scapegoat. How can you blame Jesus for your open sin against Him? Mocking the name of Jesus does not bode well for modern man! He has friends in Heavenly places.

Theses horns of power speak from heaven and say, "Loose the four angels who are bound at the great river Euphrates."

The boundary between Babylon and Jerusalem was the Euphrates River. A desert lies to the east of the Jordan River. Attacks from Babylon moved North, up the Euphrates, then down from the North, into Jerusalem. The enemies of the Children of Israel were known as the Kings of the North. The river Euphrates begins in Turkey. Modern day Turkey recently claimed the waters of the Euphrates and built a dam. The water dried up natural pools around Baghdad. It is no longer easy to fish for free food.

"And the sixth angel poured out his vial upon the great river Euphrates; and the water thereof was dried up, that the way of the kings of the east might be prepared." (Revelation 16:12).

Maxwell was ending his book, Gods Cares II on Revelation. He sensed a day would come when the river Euphrates, would dry up. This seemed to amuse him. In his day, shepherds could cross the Euphrates with their sheep. In the Iraq war the army moved easily over the Euphrates on pontoon bridges.

But more likely the way to prepare for the kings of the East is not about crossing desert or water. The Kings of the East, are words chosen to denote, the place where the Kings of Heaven come from. The East, they come from the direction of the Sun. When I think of masses of angels gathering in a moment between us and the sun, they could blot out the face of the sun. Their mass would cast a shadow over the earth to create a dark day without sun or star light. It would seem the stars had fallen and lost their light. It will create fear or joy!

Perhaps the weather, snow or rain gives us time to think of what we cannot see, beyond Orion's Gates. The Horsehead Nebula seems like a perfect icon for Heaven. The beast Michael rides, among us, defending us, protecting us with his unseen angels is a white horse.

Michael Reavels His Army Of Angels

"And the numbers of the army of the horsemen were two hundred thousand, thousand [200,000,000]: and I heard the number of them. And thus I saw the horses in the vision, and them that sat on them, having breastplates of fire, and of jacinth, and brimstone: and the heads of the horses were as the heads of lions; and out of their mouths issued fire and smoke and brimstone. By these three was the third part of men killed, by the fire, and by the smoke, and by the brimstone, which issued out of their mouths. *For their power is in their mouth, and in their tails: for their tails were like unto serpents, and had heads, and with them they do hurt.* (Revelation 9:16-19).

Adam and Eve were deceived by a snake. Who do we blame when *we are deceived by the one who seeks to destroy, deceive and confuse the very elect*? When Lucifer turns loose his anger, he releases plagues, wind, hail, sickness and destruction. Why blame God? He warned us about Lucifer, rebelling and vexing his Holy Spirit! You want to serve Lucifer? You want the enemy as a friend? Not me!

"And *the rest of the men which were not killed by these plagues yet repented not* of the works of their hands, that they should not worship devils, and idols of gold, and silver, and brass, and stone, and of wood: which neither can see, nor hear, nor walk: Neither repented they of their murders, nor of their sorceries, nor of their fornication, nor of their thefts. (Revelation 9:20–21 emphasis added)

The World will not change. Worldlings refuse to repent, of their murders, sorceries, fornication and thefts. God moved his people away from Mount Sinai. Once men feared God and his Thunder as the sound of his Trumpet got louder and louder.

The builder of a city, not made by human hands is the New Jerusalem, not a wild speculation. Eight point five billion planets are identified as likely to support life. (TIME, November 18,

2013). The Orion Nebula delivers colors that support life, while out of Orion galaxies, stars and moons are born. Life outside our Planet is real. Michael is real! Michael's army of angels are real and superior in number and strength. Even the devil trembles at the thought!

Suppose we start a new colony on Mars? Will we find harmony with God and man? Or will lawlessness prevail? What have we learned when men live without a moral compass? Riot and ruin!

Chapter XI

The Seventh Angel Sounds We Recognize Jesus Christ As Michael Has Been Victorious Over Lucifer And Babylon!

"But in the days of the voice of the seventh angel, when he shall begin to sound, the mystery of God should be finished, as he hath declared to his servants the prophets." (Revelation 10:7).

The angel is Jesus Christ, in Revelation 10:10. He stands with one foot on the sea and one foot on the land, showing he has authority over all the earth. "And he said unto me. Thou must prophesy again before many peoples, and nations, and tongues, and kings."

And you ask me why I dare publish a book that must prophesy again before many peoples, nations and languages, and kings? Should I deny this command? Who do I fear? Who shall I be afraid of? Whose side are you on? Lucifer is trembling with fear!

Chapter XII

Heaven Is Opened The Red Horse Appears

"And I saw when the **Lamb opened one of the seals**, and I heard, as it were the noise of thunder, one of the four beasts saying, Come and see. And **I saw, and behold a white horse:** and he that sat on him had a bow; and a crown was given unto him: and he went forth conquering, and to conquer. And when he had opened the second seal, I heard the second beast say, Come and see. And there went out another **horse that was red**: and power was given to him that sat thereon to take peace from the earth, and that they should kill one another: and there was given unto him a great sword. (Revelation 6:1-4).

"And **I saw heaven opened,** and behold a white horse; and he that sat upon him [The White Horse] was called Faithful and True, and in righteousness he doth judge and make war." (Revelation 19:11).

HEAVEN IS OPEN!

"His eyes were as a flame of fire, and on his head were many crowns; and **he had a name written, that no man knew, but he himself.**" (Revelation 19:12).

By opening the 7th Seal, the 7 Angels are sounding, Jesus Christ is Our High Priest known as Michael the Archangel who has won over Lucifer.

Michael sits on his Red Horse watching his enemies kill his enemies. He is stuck there. He cannot move backward, he cannot move forward. God is not silent. Heaven is in expectancy...of what will happen next

Babylon has fallen, now the kings of the earth and their armies, gathered to make war against Michael who sits on the horse. But, Jesus has already conquered Lucifer at the cross.

"And I saw the beast, and the kings of the earth, and their armies, gathered together to make war against him that sat on the horse, and against his army." (Revelation 19:19).

Jesus reigns over the earth and who can withstand His wrath?

"Who is man that Thou art mindful of him?"

"Out of the mouth of babes and sucklings hast thou ordained strength because of thine enemies, that thou mightest still the enemy and the avenger.

"When I consider thy heavens, the work of thy fingers, the moon and the stars, which thou hast ordained; What is man, that thou art mindful of him? and the son of man, that thou visitest him? For thou hast made him a little lower than the angels, and hast crowned him with glory and honour.

"Thou madest him to have dominion over the works of thy hands; thou hast put all things under his feet: All sheep and oxen, yea, and the beasts of the field; The fowl of the air, and the fish of the sea, and whatsoever passeth through the paths of the seas.

"O LORD our Lord, how excellent is thy name in all the earth!" (Psalms 8:2-9).

Who has your vote? Michael or Lucifer?

Chapter XIII

Ellen White Prophecies Being Fulfilled And Yet To Be Fulfilled:

There are two prophecies yet to be fulfilled according to Ellen G. White (1827-1915) and the Temple Institute is in agreement.

1.) "*When God's temple in heaven* is opened, what a triumphant time that will be for all who have been faithful and true! In the [heavenly] temple will be seen the ark of the testament in which were placed the two tables of stone, on which are written God's law. These tables of stone will be brought forth from their hiding place, and on them, will be seen the Ten Commandments engraved by the finger of God. **These tables of stone now lying in the ark of the testament will be a convincing testimony to the truth and binding claims of God's law.**" (Letter 47, 1902) Ellen White Comments: on Revelation 11, SDA Bible Commentary p. 972, Volume 7.

"And I saw heaven opened, and behold a white horse; and he that sat upon him was called Faithful and True, and in righteousness he doth judge and make war." (Revelation 19:11).

In order to complete Gods will, he wants to teach us to know he can and will destroy those who destroy the earth. The Covenant made on Mt. Sinai, was his wedding vow to you, His Bride, His Church. He sends Michael to protect and defend all who call upon the name of the Lord!

Lucifer seeks to change the times and laws of God. If there is no punishment of sin, against God, Jesus would not have to die. Lucifer caused Jesus to die, influenced Judas his disciple to take a bribe, and influenced two High Priests, to offer the blood of an innocent man to die, to protect themselves from Rome. Priests used Pilate and the

Roman Government to do what they could not do. Without the Roman Government they had no authority to murder Jesus and his followers. Behind laws to exterminate people is The Destroyer, Lucifer, the fallen angel.

Prophecy was fulfilled. Jesus is the Son of God, and he lived to see religion become corrupt by attempting to unite the church, *to use civil laws to defend their "religious beliefs."*

Spiritual laws are for people who have a spiritual connection to the Holy Spirit. The will of God on earth is the will of God in Heaven. If we war against the Government of God now, we would never be happy in heaven with God then. Heaven would be a miserable place for wicked men who wish to destroy the happiness of others!

If we don't want to bow down and worship Our Creator now, then we must understand *created beings cannot be the Creator.* The controversy with God is his wrath against men who rebel and vex his Holy Spirit. We come to the judgment of the living. "If there be a controversy between men, and they come unto judgment, that the judges may judge them; then they shall justify the righteous, and condemn the wicked." (Deuteronomy 25:1). Wow! God is on our side! Love God hate sin! They will not mock him!

The Jewish Temple Institute agrees, in Gods time the Ten Commandments will be revealed and come out of hiding. God wills our first duty is to glorify him, his character, and Gods Sanctuary in the New Jerusalem. The promise to Abraham is for all nations to be received on the Temple Mount, to learn about God, who sent his son to be the blood sacrifice. How barbarian is a human blood sacrifice?

The Orthodox Jews are cautious. The Church State Government of Iran wants to place their Caliph on the Temple Mount. Will they accept a Church/State religion? Can a man dictate who we pray too? Is Allah God? Do we want one man to control our states and spiritual justice? Or will we be satisfied with our unseen God and his son? Have we found contentment in the Holy Spirit?

2.) "Study the 9th chapter of Ezekiel, These words will be literally fulfilled; yet the time is passing, and the people are asleep. They refuse to humble their souls and to be converted. Not a great while longer will the Lord bear with the people who have such great and important truths revealed to them, but who refuse to bring these truths into their individual experience. The time is short. God is calling; will you hear? Will you receive His message? Will you be converted before it is too late? Soon, very soon, every case will be decided for eternity." (Letter 106, 1909. Manuscript Release No. 59—3.)

GOD TOLD EZEKIEL HOW THE TEMPLE MOUNT WILL BE TAKEN.

"He cried also in mine ears with a loud voice, saying, Cause them that have charge over the city to draw near, even every man *with* his destroying weapon in his hand.

"And, behold, six men came from the way of the higher gate, which lieth toward the north, and every man a slaughter weapon in his hand; and one man among them *was* clothed with linen, with a writer's inkhorn by his side: and they went in, and stood beside the brazen altar. And the glory of the God of Israel was gone up from the cherub, whereupon he was, to the threshold of the house. And he called to the man clothed with linen, which *had* the writer's inkhorn by his side; And the LORD said unto him, Go through the midst of the city, through the midst of Jerusalem, and **set a mark upon the foreheads of the men that sigh and that cry for all the abominations that be done in the midst thereof.** And to the others he said in mine hearing, Go ye after him through the city, and smite: let not your eye spare, neither have ye pity**: Slay utterly old *and* young, both maids, and little children, and women: but come not near any man upon whom *is* the mark; and begin at my sanctuary.** Then they began at the ancient men which *were* before the house. [**The light of the Presence of the Lord, on the**

Day of Atonement, would devour a man with sin in his heart. That same power will devour instantly, men who cherish pride, greed and extortion.] And he said unto them, Defile the house, and fill the courts with the slain: go ye forth. And they went forth, and slew in the city. And it came to pass, while they were slaying them, and I was left, that I fell upon my face, and cried, and said, Ah Lord GOD! wilt thou destroy all the residue of Israel in thy pouring out of thy fury upon Jerusalem? Then said he unto me, **The iniquity of the house of Israel and Judah *is* exceeding great, and the land is full of blood, and the city full of perverseness: for they say, The LORD hath forsaken the earth, and the LORD seeth not.** And as for me also, mine eye shall not spare, neither will I have pity, *but* I will recompense their way upon their head. **And, behold, the man clothed with linen, which *had* the inkhorn by his side, reported the matter, saying, I have done as thou hast commanded me."**

(Ezekiel 9:1-11)

"Set a mark upon the foreheads of the men [and women] that sigh and cry for all the abominations that be done!"

God has heard the prayers of those who cry! Opening the 7th Seal, by the 7th Angel is his response, to expose the devil and those who attempt to sit on His Throne. Michael stands up to vindicate his prophets.

"And he causeth all, both small and great, rich and poor, free and bond, to receive a mark in their right hand, or in their foreheads: And that no man might buy or sell, save he that had the mark, or the name of the beast, or the number of his name." (Revelation 13:16,17).

It doesn't take a rocket scientist to know the *benefits* of a government who can label you with a number and G.P.S. tracking system. *Then you can feel secure in the arms of a computer?*

John wrote in 95 A.D. of the day, you would be called to place your heart to a vote! 100 % in love with Jesus, depending on God and his universe to cheer you on! We cannot imagine the watchers and the Holy ones, who tried to awaken us to truth.

After the fall of Jerusalem in 70 A.D. John was persecuted, they tried to fry in him oil, but he wouldn't die. He was banished to the Island of Patmos. And this is what makes this prophecy so powerful. *Martyrdom will not save one soul now that Jesus has left the Heavenly Sanctuary.* No church can pardon sin against God! A church that condones sin tends to give license to evil. Heavy is the yoke which the carnal heart is willing to bear rather than bow down to the yoke of the Creator. His burden is easy, his yoke is light!

The fall of Jerusalem in 70 A.D. could not be in the prophecy written in 95 A.D. when *judgment comes to Gods House.* And if judgment comes first to Gods House, then what will be the judgment on those who have never heard of the forgiving goodness of God? Will we cry when we find we forgot to warn our family and friends? When the thieves were dying, one thief said, "Jesus is innocent."

Daniel stand up. The Heavenly Courts have turned the rulership of the world over to the Saints of the Most High God. Daniel 7. He sifts the grain from the chaff.

A PROPHETESS GIVES US REASSURANCE.

June 20, 1903: "There are many with whom the Spirit of God is striving. The time of God's destructive judgment is the time of mercy for those who have no opportunity to learn what is truth. Tenderly will the Lord look upon them. His heart of mercy is touched; His hand is still out stretched out to save." Life Sketches p. 412 Ellen White

Under the date of August 3, 1903, Mrs. White further wrote regarding a sensational report: "How comes the word that I have declared that New York is to be swept away by a tidal wave? This I have never said. I have said, as I looked at the great building going up there, story after story; 'What terrible scenes will take place when the Lord shall arise to shake terribly the earth! Then the words of Revelation 18:1-3 will be fulfilled.' The whole of the eighteenth chapter of Revelation is a warning of what is coming on the earth.

But I have no light in particular in regard to what is coming on New York., only I know that one day the great buildings there will be thrown down by the turning and overturning of the Lord, one touch of His mighty, power, and these massive structures will fall. Scenes will take place the fearfulness of which we cannot image."(*Life Sketches* p. 411-412 Ellen White).

True prophets point us back to the Bible. A careful look at Revelation 18 confirms what the Bible says. Revelation18, reveals Michael has stood up having great power, and the earth is lightened with his glory. He cries out to get us out of Babylon, out of confusion. All have drunk the wine of her wrath her lies and we are called to "Come out of her, my people, that ye be not partakers of her sins, and that ye receive not of her plagues." In verse twenty there is rejoicing on earth that corresponds to the rejoicing in heaven! "Rejoice over her, *thou* heaven, and *ye* holy apostles and prophets; for God hath avenged you on her. But there is a sad reminder in the last paragraph. "And in her was found the blood of prophets, and of saints, and of all that were slain upon the earth." (Revelation 18:24).

If you are in the false church that kills the prophets and saints, you will also kill the prophet John, who wrote this in 95 A.D. some twenty years after the judgment on Jerusalem, as predicted by Jesus, The Prophet. If you are in the Remnant Church of those who follow Jesus, you will see Michael stand up, calling us out of confusion, to see the judgment on the Jews happened in 70 A.D. This judgment is on the Christians, like you and me. The gifts of the Holy Spirit are being poured out and will continue with healings and supernatural manifestations, as God has promised.

"And at that time shall Michael stand up, the great prince which standeth for the children of thy people: and there shall be a time of trouble, such as never was since there was a nation *even* to that same time: and at that time thy people shall be delivered, every one that shall be found written in the book. *And many of them that sleep in the dust of the earth shall awake, some to everlasting life, and some to shame and everlasting contempt.* And they that be wise shall shine as the brightness of the firmament; and they that turn many to righteousness as the stars for ever and ever. But thou, O Daniel, shut up the words, and seal the book, *even* to the time of the end: many shall run to and fro, and knowledge shall be increased. (Daniel 12:1-4).

When the dead rise from their graves, from Adam and Eve to Noah, and his seed, we will hear and see the vision of Daniel come alive in our day! This is the first resurrection. The earth will open up, to let out those who slept in the peace of sleep, waiting for Jesus to raise the dead with the sound of the Arch angel. He comforts us by the great reality of being able to raise the dead. Not just your family, but Gods Family from the beginning of the day, Adam and Eve were forced out of the Garden of Eden for their sin of obeying Lucifer, the snake. That ate the forbidden fruit, forever a reminder of being shut out from the presence of God and His Holy Spirit. This is the day we will see those who have died being loyal to their royal connection to Jesus a Jew, the Lamb of God.

An asteroid attack may happen, but God is not in the business of destroying, Lucifer is. The attack on New York and Washington D.C. was done by a handful of men, most likely about twenty. Had they achieved their goal of watching the Twin Towers tumble over into Wall Street, the loss of lives would certainly be higher. Each tower could accommodate fifty thousand souls. One hundred thousand employees, and staff, could have reached a death toll, far beyond, the under three thousand lives that were lost. Had they not "melted like pitch," as prophesied in 1903, 9-11-2001 could have been far more destructive. How did God know *how the buildings would melt in 1903? Prophecy proves the Bible is true!*

"In India, China, Russia, and the cities of America, thousands of men and women are dying of starvation. The moneyed men, because they have the power, control the market. They purchase at low rates all they can obtain, and then sell at greatly increased prices. This means starvation to the poorer classes, and will result in a civil war. There will be a time of trouble such as never as since there was a nation. *And at that time shall Michael stand up, the great prince which standeth for the children of thy people:* and there shall be a time of trouble such as never was since there was a nation, even to that same time; *and at that time thy people shall be delivered, everyone that shall be found written in the book* . . .Many shall be purified, and made white, and tried; but the wicked shall do wickedly, and none of the wicked shall understand, but the wise shall understand." (MS 114, 1899. MR No. 325 1899).

God saw the Kingdoms on earth, controlling the stock markets. In spite of people dying of starvation in their own countries, they would make a profit. However, when Michael stands up, Gods people will be delivered! Many will be purified and made whole, and tried. The wicked will not understand, but the wise will understand. These are ones who have a heart of compassion for Jesus Christ. They love their Saviour, even unto death.

ON THE PLAGUES SHE WROTE:

And "the rivers and fountains of waters . . . became blood." Terrible as these inflictions are, **God's justice stands fully vindicated.** The angel of God declares: **"Thou hast judged thus. For they have shed the blood of saints and prophets, and Thou hast given them blood to drink; for they are worthy."** Revelation 16:2-6. By condemning the people of God to death, they have as truly incurred the guilt of their blood as if it had been shed by their hands. **In like manner Christ declared the Jews of His time guilty of all the blood of holy men which had been shed since the day of Abel; for they possessed the same spirit and were seeking to do the same work with these murderers of the prophets."** (Great Controversy 627-629).

Among The Rebukes Of Ellen White Is This Statement:

"The third angel's message is the most solemn, fearful, and important. To us God has entrusted it, and we are accountable for the way we handle this sacred testing truth. If our defects of character betray us into sins which repulse souls and turn them from the truth, their blood will be upon our garments." (Letter 1, 1873, p. 10).

We may have *more knowledge* by being exposed to truth. However Ellen White feared the Bible and her writings would be used as a club, to destroy, instead of a means to edify and enlighten each other.

Symbols:

In this quick guide to symbols, we have found angels both good and bad, kingdoms both good and bad, and always sheep that go astray, and need the Good Shepherd. Teaching takes patience and time for the tender sprouts to grow wise. We will all know good from evil before it is too late.

Symbols separate the good from evil. Under Lucifer you have the destroyer who counterfeits everything good. Under Jesus you have the open arms of a Mother, who realizes we may learn best by the things we suffer. The Mother winches to see her child take the wounds of learning to walk but her wisdom proves this too will change. Someday the child will become a man and too will watch his child learn to stand, walk and run and perhaps learn to fly a kite at the same time.

Stay in touch. Let me hear a good word from you! Let me know you are learning new symbols and finding it easier to know Jesus and God. "Blessed are the poor in Spirit, theirs is the Kingdom of Heaven!"

"For I know the plans that I have for you, 'declares the LORD', plans for well-being, and not for calamity, in order to give you a future and a hope. When you call out to me and come and pray to me, I'll hear you. You will seek me and find me when you search for me with all your heart." (Jeremiah 29:11-13)

"And in her [the false church, Babylon] was found the blood of prophets, and of saints, and of all that were slain upon the earth. (Revelation 18:24).

"The Spirit and the bride say, "Come!" Let everyone who hears this say, "Come!" Let everyone who is thirsty come! Let anyone who wants the water of life take it as a gift!" (Revelation 22:17 ISV).

May the Lord bless and keep you and may his face always shine upon you and give you peace!

As fate would have it, I watched the blood moon last night. I saw a pink moon hung in the sky like a ball on a Christmas Tree. I would love to look out my window and see such a sight again. And with Jesus I would like to think we could into the unity of faith, finding in the Fourth Commandment our Creator. In the Seventh Commandment I would like to think we could find Jesus Christ as the missing link in our genealogy the father, the mother, the brother or sister we have lost contact with for many reasons. Faith in the blood of Jesus as my salvation who gives me courage to put on the helmet of salvation, the breastplate of His Righteousness, the Sword of Truth is not always my nature to hold like a foil. But truth cuts deeply into the problem of how I run away or stand up to defend Jesus. My nature is to run away from trouble, confusion, and even dialog, that seems to me, puts a curse on the name "discussion." I want the boots or shoes that are made for me to wear as I cross the world to defend the name of Jesus. And all this I learned from my Aunt Twila in Sabbath School as a very young child.

If you have not had my training and the Sword, the Helmet, the Breastplate and shoes, then you might start out barefoot and walk through the Garden of Eden with Adam and Eve in Genesis. Or you might want to cross over the Jordan with those who finally came to rest in the Promised Land called Canaan. I've been there in the Promised Land, and I wonder who wants to fight over that rock pile, and rock streets, and rock houses, how could anyone forget the THE ROCK is Jesus. We are fighting for Him to be the Head of His Church?

I hope that I will not be guilty of judging anyone ever! It is bad enough to feel the damage that occurs when I have been misjudged. I would not wish that on you or anyone! Presenting the TRUTH and nothing but THE TRUTH, is like carrying a sword that might hurt someone's feelings. And as I side step the issue of truth, it keeps coming back to hunt me! Did God really say, not everyone would be happy in heaven? I often wondered who would be the first to pick a fight once they got to heaven? Really? If you had thousand years or more to live, what would it matter if someone wants your job? Let him do the work. Let her take care of the children. Let them wax the car.

This thing of time and space giving us time to finish off the planet with a few more tons of rubbish, and waste, is mind boggling. If Lucifer had more time to destroy, what would be left of the Universe? Was it wise for God to make this planet as the very last reality game to prove pride, greed and using others as our slaves, is not something we want in Heaven? I can understand why the folks in heaven are celebrating. Even the heavenly beings have seen enough of the lies initiated by Lucifer. Why can't I say, "I've had enough! Let GOD destroy the created being that went ballistic! Let the devil die a death in boiling oil? Did I say that? Isn't that how they tried to silence the voice of John the Revelator? Didn't they try to boil him in oil? Oh, what Lucifer has to look forward too! All the plots and schemes he planned to destroy the Law and Prophets has come to an end.

I will not dwell on the problems of thinking mean thoughts, even against the one who brings them to mind. I will dwell on a city called the New Jerusalem with a river running through it, that we can walk across without a thought. I will like to think of days skating on a sea of glass, or going under water to play with dolphins. I would rather end my day imaging a walk with Jesus through a tropical forest with a giraffe peeking out from the boughs, and a monkey heckling Jesus by riding on his neck. A banana might come in helpful to feed that monkey. Creativity will abound, all around us, with signs and wonders we will be lost in a spell of turning around and around to try and take it all in. Mesmerized by the sights, sounds, and smells we cannot imagine. I want to touch a furry bear and walk with him to a river. I want to see a baby curled up next to a snake in safety. I want the *fear* of living and being in heaven, be the thoughts I have when I go to sleep. I want the fear of God to shake me up and turn me around to see, He holds the future in His hands, and that includes you and me.

I don't know what else I can say to convince you of your commitment to not tell a lie about why Jesus died at the hands of his family and friends? We are a motley crew aboard this ship on the seas of life. Sometimes I even wonder about you. Worse yet I wonder about myself? Are we really on the same side? Or have we broken our commitment to let Jesus lead everyone to where they need to be, with or without my help?

Is it I? The disciples asked when Jesus said, "One among you is going to betray me." Will I be replaced if I fail to rightly represent my Jesus as the one who loves you and me? I like Peter would like to say, "I will defend you Jesus with my life!" And what will I say when the prophecy comes true and we will not be able to buy or sell unless I take the mark in my right hand or forehead?

Great Grandma Anderson had it all worked out. When a robber would break in she would say, "Can I get you something to eat." When a police man would pull her over and ask for her driver's license, she planned to say, "Lock me up officer." I guess when the times comes I might try to trade a peach for a pardon. But the word is out, we might have to start growing our own gardens and weeding them too.

Being without money, will lead us to barter and having food in the garden is an easy way to make friends and enjoy the neighbors. I would wish you all five acres and seeds to watch grow. Being without meat is not the worst possible scenario. A potato is among the few foods that will keep you alive it even has Vitamin C. Farmers know they can plant the seed but *the breeze,* the sun, the moon, and rain is needed to make plant healthy. And when we get out in the breeze, sun and moon we too can work and feel accomplished in finishing a bit of weeding, while we wait for the wedding party to meet our Bridegroom Jesus.

If Jesus can wait on his Red Horse for us to bless those who come in his name, I can wait, but surely I would want to bless you for coming in the name of the Lord, to study a book, dedicated to honor his name and character. Then "whosoever calls upon the name of the Lord shall be saved." (Romans 10:13). Then the only ones left will be the devil and his angels. And they already know their future. Their sitting on death row.

Contact:
Connie@DecodingBibleProphecy.com
(855) 334-9097

P.S. Walter's story is on the website. He has been challenged with his own mission to go to Israel and walk in the footsteps of Jesus with his friend Dorren who has studied at the International House of Prayer. You might want to follow their journey on facebook. They leave May 3, 2014.

Walter is writing a book called *GOD me. I hope to get his permission to put it up on this website when it is finished.*

P.S. God still has men, women and children who are open to the Holy Spirit, and they are having visions and dreams. Yesterday, my Mother woke up around 3 a.m. She saw pictures of people, who were dead. There was a good looking man with dark hair, his wife's name was Hillary. She is a widow and she is contemplating if she can trust 100% in Jesus as her Messiah. I don't know who you are. I only know that God and Jesus love and understand the widows. You are not alone! Jesus is the good guy and Lucifer is the destroyer of everything good. That is why Jesus died for you! He loves you! And He can protect you from the seen and unseen forces, by just saying, "I'm saved by the blood of the Lamb, Jesus Christ is My Saviour." The devil fears and trembles because he knows how many he sent to the fiery furnaces and that is where we want this evil force to go. God bless you and keep you, and carry you if necessary.